# Contents

Some words are shown in bold, **like this**.
You can find them in the glossary on page 23.

# What is red?

Red is a colour.

What different colours can you see in this picture?

The colour red is all around.

What do you do with these red things?

# What red things can I eat?

Strawberries are good to eat.

When they are red, we can pick and eat them.

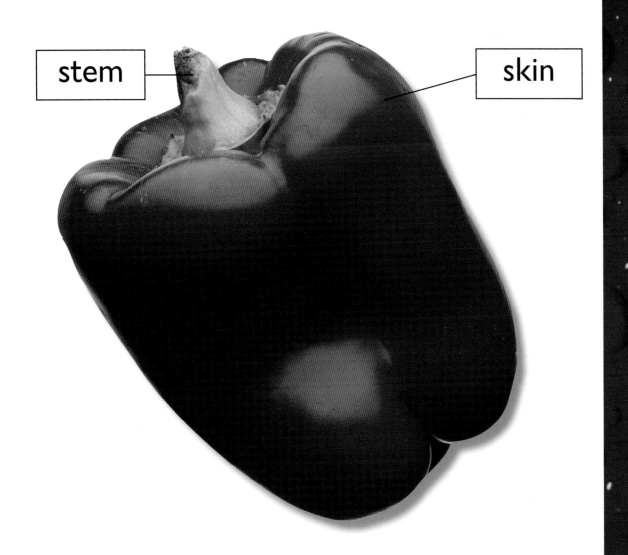

stem

skin

Some peppers are red.

They have red **skin** and a green **stem**.

# What red clothes can I wear?

This shirt is made of red **cotton**.

Cotton keeps you cool.

These red mittens are made of **wool**.

Wool keeps your hands warm.

# What is red on buildings?

Some buildings are made of red bricks.

Bricks are hard and strong.

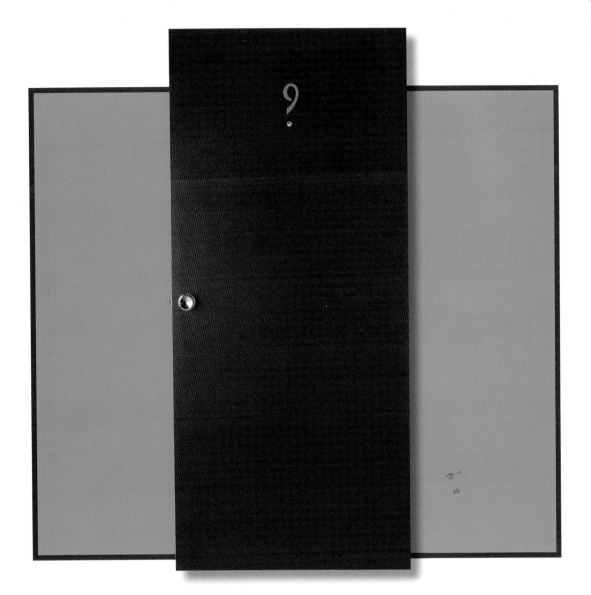

This front door is red.

It is made of wood and painted red.

# What is red at home?

handle grips

seat

This tricycle is red.

It has a red seat and handle grips.

This mug is red.

It keeps the cocoa hot.

# Can I find red things in a city?

These traffic lights are sometimes red.

When the light is red, traffic must stop.

This fire engine is red.

It is used to fight fires.

# Can I find red things in a forest?

Red **berries** grow in a forest.

They are easy to see in the snow.

The **leaves** of this tree are red.

Some leaves turn red in autumn.

# Are there red animals?

Red animals live in gardens.

Ladybirds are red insects.

Red animals live in the sea.

This starfish is red and yellow.

# How do people celebrate with red?

People **celebrate** Chinese New Year with lots of red.

They put up red lanterns.

People celebrate with fireworks.

Red fireworks look good in the night sky.

# Quiz

What red things can you see?

Look for the answers on page 24.

# Glossary

**berries**
small, round, juicy fruit

**celebrate**
do something special to show a day or event is important

**cotton**
material made from the cotton plant; used to make clothes

**leaves**
flat parts of a plant that grow from the stem or a branch

**skin**
the outer layer of vegetables or fruit

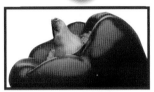

**stem**
the centre part of a plant

**wool**
thread made from soft hair of sheep; used to make clothes

# Index

Answers to the quiz on page 22

paint   smock

table

chairs

## Notes to parents and teachers

Reading non-fiction texts for information is an important part of a child's literacy development. Readers can be encouraged to ask simple questions and then use the text to find the answers. Each chapter in this book begins with a question. Read the questions together. Look at the pictures. Talk about what the answer might be. Then read the text to find out if your predictions were correct. To develop readers' enquiry skills, encourage them to think of other questions they might ask about the topic. Discuss where you could find the answers. Assist children in using the contents page, picture glossary and index to practise research skills and new vocabulary.